MW01644291

# WEALTH BEYOND WORK

Achieving Financial Freedom In
Your Golden Years

ALLEN THOMAS

Allen Thomas
e.allenthomas@me.com
https://thomasadvisoryservices.com/

Wealth Beyond Work, Allen Thomas —1st ed.

# TESTIMONIALS

"Allen is the consummate professional. We recently transitioned from full-time private practice to semi-retirement. Allen listened carefully during our discussions about financial needs, and then he got busy finding investment vehicles that meet our current and long-term goals. He is always available when we have questions or concerns, and he patiently explains the portions of our financial picture that we don't naturally understand. And he gets the results he promises! Couldn't ask for a more conscientious and engaged financial advisor."

**Kerry and Kelly Brown**

"We have known Allen Thomas and his family for almost 20 years. Allen has handled our retirement funds for 16 years. Allen carefully identified us as conservative investors and has maintained that goal. We are pleased with the personal attention given to us by Allen and his staff. We highly recommend Allen Thomas, Financial Advisor."

**Dot and Lamar Sims**

"In our community center lobby, we spotted a brochure for an upcoming financial presentation by Allen Thomas. We went to the presentation and we were impressed, so we decided to work with Allen. He has worked very closely with us, advising us about all of our financial needs. We have been very satisfied with Allen's financial strategies."

**Ed and Donna Helfrey**

"Allen is a wonderful, intelligent man who knows his business, and his experience in his field is outstanding."

**Ed Kriso, Sr.**

"In 2023, I had a CD account maturing. I met with Allen to discuss my options to invest the money for retirement. I spent about two hours in his office going over my options. It has been over a year since I made the investment, and I am very satisfied with what Allen did for me."

**Ted Lyons**

"It's a privilege to recommend Allen to anyone who needs his services as a financial advisor. We have grown much more than we expected in the beginning by using his expert advice. We hope that all of his clients will get the beautiful results that we have! Allen went the extra mile to keep up with our needs."

**George and Barbara Phillips**

"Allen Thomas is one of the most kind and generous people I know. He is helpful to everyone, both in business and with his friends, family, and church community. He is quick to help you with any problem you may have. He stays on top of things when taking care of my business needs. I feel very fortunate to have him in my life and as my financial advisor. God has blessed me with knowing Allen."

**Julia Smith**

"We have been clients of Allen Thomas for many years. Being a fiduciary financial advisor, Allen always asks the right questions to be able to invest our funds to benefit us for the future. We are grateful for the rider on our policies, and income for life. This has been very helpful to us now, as we use the extra monthly income to help with our bills. We would like for Allen to know just how much we appreciate him, his knowledge, thoughtfulness, and caring for us over all these years."

**Bobby and Marcia Crawford**

# DEDICATION

I dedicate this book to my parents, Gordon E. Thomas and Irma M. Thomas, for their wisdom, knowledgeable teachings, Godly approach to my upbringing, and for inspiring me to share these thoughts with you. Thank you, Mom & Dad.

# CONTENTS

# INTRODUCTION

Retirement is supposed to be a time of joy and fulfillment—the reward for a lifetime of hard work. Yet for many people, the dream of a secure retirement can feel distant or even out of reach. There's an understandable reason for this: financial planning can be complex and, at times, overwhelming. It involves a maze of decisions, regulations, and calculations that can feel confusing to many people. For those who are already busy with careers, families, and the other responsibilities of life, finding the time to develop a thoughtful plan for retirement can feel impossible. But the truth is, the earlier you start, the more secure you'll feel about what lies ahead.

As a financial planner, I've had countless conversations with clients about the fears and anxieties that come with financial planning. I understand the worries that keep people up at night, as well as the confusion that causes many people to delay making important decisions. If you've experienced these feelings, I want you to know that you're not alone—and that there's a way to simplify the process. Financial planning doesn't have to be complicated or fill you with stress. With the right approach, you can address each part of your financial picture thoughtfully and create a solid foundation that will carry you into retirement with confidence. This book was written to make that process easier for people like you. My goal is to help you simplify, organize, and understand the essential elements of financial planning so that you can feel secure in the choices you make.

As you go through this book, you'll discover that planning for retirement isn't just about numbers—it's about knowing that your future will be secure and that your family will be taken care of. It's about building a solid foundation that leaves you prepared for the unknown. Whether you're just beginning to think about retirement or are already well into the planning stages, this book is designed to guide you through every step of the journey.

While financial planning is often seen as something you "get around to later," it's one of the most powerful investments of time and effort that you can make. In my experience, the earlier people start, the more they are able to accomplish. But no matter where you are in the process, it's never too late to start taking steps to secure your future.

## Why Financial Planning Matters

Financial planning is more than just setting aside money or choosing investments. It's about gaining clarity and confidence in your decisions, knowing that you're laying the foundation for a comfortable retirement. But the stakes are high. Without a thoughtful plan, you might find yourself facing unnecessary financial stress, missing opportunities to grow your retirement income, or even running out of money during retirement.

One of the greatest benefits of a well-organized plan is the peace of mind that comes from knowing your financial future is under control. With the right foundation, you'll know that you're making informed decisions and protecting yourself from risks that could undermine your retirement. You'll be better equipped to handle life's uncertainties, manage debt effectively, and understand how to turn your assets into a steady income. When you have a plan in place, you're in the driver's seat, able to anticipate and adapt to whatever life throws your way.

## Why I Wrote This Book

Over my years as a financial planner, I've seen too many people struggle with the complexities of retirement planning. They come to me unsure of where to begin, often feeling overwhelmed and uncertain about what's involved. I've witnessed firsthand the relief that comes when someone finally understands their options, and I've seen the confidence that grows when people see a clear path forward.

That's why I created this book: to demystify the financial planning process and offer you a straightforward approach. This book is designed to take you step-by-step through the essential areas of retirement planning so that you can approach each stage with clarity and confidence. I'll introduce you to **The Four Pillars**, a 4-step financial planning process that I built to simplify your financial journey. Along the way, I'll provide clear guidance and actionable advice on the aspects of planning that matter most for your future.

By the end of this book, you'll have the knowledge to confidently meet with a financial advisor and begin the process of planning for your financial future. When it comes time to make important choices about Social Security, Medicare, retirement accounts, and estate planning, you'll be prepared with the information you need to make the right decisions with an advisor's guidance.

If you're ready to take the first step toward securing your financial future, this book will serve as your guide. Whether you're planning for retirement now or are decades away from it, the work you do today will make all the difference. This book is here to provide support, guidance, and reassurance every step of the way.

Now, let's begin the journey to a retirement that is not only secure but filled with joy and blessings. With each chapter, you'll be one step closer to building the financial foundation that will carry you confidently into the future.

## CHAPTER 1

# The Never-Ending Pile of Mail

*"The journey of a thousand miles begins with one step."*

–Lao Tzu

When I ask new clients what keeps them up at night, many of them tell me the same story: "Well, I have this overflowing stack of papers. The mail comes in, and I just put all the financial paperwork aside because I'm not sure what to do with it. It just keeps piling up, and I don't understand what I even need to be taking care of or thinking about. I know I should take care of it, but I've been putting it off for so long that I'm overwhelmed by how much there is to do, and I don't know where to start."

Sometimes, these people are widows or widowers whose spouses took care of the household's finances. Now that their spouse has passed away, they feel lost…

They put the mail on the counter, thinking, "I'll deal with that soon." Yet time passes, and they continue to delay taking action. The longer they wait, the taller the stack of papers gets.

Walking past this pile of papers every day causes enormous stress… Especially as people get older and draw closer to retirement.

Do you have a never-ending pile of mail somewhere in your house?

This pile of mail is just the physical manifestation of the overwhelming number of financial decisions we all have to make in life, especially as we near retirement.

When it comes to planning for retirement, fear of the unknown keeps many people from taking action. It's easy for people to feel confused, stressed out, and unsure of where to begin…

Let's discuss some of the decisions and challenges that many people (and likely you) are facing or will face as they near traditional retirement age.

## Trying to Figure Out Medicare and Social Security

If you're not familiar with the process of setting up Medicare and Social Security, trying to navigate this step of planning for retirement can be confusing…

Most people don't know that they need a Social Security account to receive Medicare. You then have to create another account to verify your identity and access the Social Security account. Once these two accounts are set up, you're able to apply for Medicare and make decisions about when you'd like to take Social Security.

When you make decisions about when to take Medicare, you need to factor in whether or not you're still working. If you're not working at 65, you can go ahead and get Parts A and B. However, if you're still working after age 65, you can only get Part A until you retire—and you need to remember to adjust your Medicare when your employment status changes.

When you qualify for Social Security, you can evaluate your financial situation and decide whether you're going to take it now or delay it so you can get a higher benefit in the future. This decision comes down to many factors in a person's life and financial situation, and it shouldn't be made hastily because **it is difficult to change your decision once it's made.**

Often, when people make decisions about Medicare and Social Security without consulting a professional, they make mistakes. A friend of mine was having Part B premiums taken out of his checking account because he was still working and he wasn't on Social Security. When he went on Social Security, the Part B premiums were automatically taken out of his Social Security. He didn't realize that he hadn't disconnected the automatic payments from his bank, so his Part B premiums were being taken out of two places. After many years, he met with me, and we realized his mistake. We were able to help him get about $20,000 back from Social Security, but Social Security will only go back so far, so he lost money. If you are in a similar situation, know that it's up to you to remember to disconnect your automatic bank payments—Social Security won't give you a letter or notification when they begin taking Medicare payments out of Social Security. If you aren't careful, like my friend, you could end up paying doubly for Medicare.

## Is Your Estate in Order?

As people near retirement, they often forget to plan for what happens to their estate after they pass away. If someone passes away without their estate in order, the estate will automatically go through probate. Creating a revocable trust and titling your assets into that trust will avoid probate for you and your heirs.

It's crucial to have beneficiaries on all of your assets. However, as you get closer to retirement age, it's time to go a step further and create a will—and keep it updated. I meet many retirees from the north who come down to Florida, bringing along the wills they created before moving. However, Florida statutes change every few years, and now, it's imperative in Florida that you have a Florida will. Retirees who don't revisit their wills with a financial planner each year would miss this change and not realize that, in Florida, they effectively don't have a will.

Many people don't know the difference between a will and a trust, and this distinction is important (we'll cover this later in the book). Essentially, a trust document avoids probate, and a will does not. Most people need some combination of the two to ensure their assets pass to their loved ones without going through probate.

Seniors should also have a power of attorney in place so that if they become incapacitated or disabled, someone they trust can make medical and financial decisions on their behalf.

When it comes to estate planning, it's important not to delay…

A client of mine delayed finalizing her estate plan for three years, despite my urging her to take action.

Finally, when she got admitted to intensive care, she called me, panicking, wanting to get her will done as soon as possible.

We got a will prepared, and I went to the intensive care unit to see her, staying from the afternoon until nearly midnight as we hurried to get signatures and finalize beneficiaries. She wanted her four children to be her beneficiaries, but she also wanted 19 other friends, relatives, and members of her church to receive some of her money. It took us hours to figure out how to make that happen, but eventually, we accomplished it.

That day, my client felt regret that she had procrastinated for so long over her estate plan. She wished she could have sorted out her estate plan in my office, with plenty of time to think through important decisions, not in an intensive care bed, rushed and worried she would not complete the plan before her condition got worse.

## Disbursements, Taxes, and Decisions Around Retirement Accounts

Where are your assets, and what does that mean in retirement?

Maybe you have a pension if you worked for the state or local government, in a role such as a teacher or law enforcement. If you have a pension, you'll need to make decisions about what to do with it, and you only get one shot at making these decisions. For instance, many people select "Life Only" because it is the default option. But "Life Only" means that the monthly benefit stops at your death. If you pass away, your spouse does not get that pension. It's important to evaluate this decision with a professional and truly understand the options you have so you select the right one for you and your family. There is no "one-size-fits-all" option, and the best option for you will depend on your unique circumstances.

On top of a pension, state employees may also have a state retirement program. You now have more options to evaluate...

I've had clients come in bragging about the new truck or boat they bought with their state retirement plan because they chose to take it as a lump sum... Until I tell them, "Well, come April, you're not going to be happy, because every bit of the income you got from that retirement plan is going to be taxed."

It's important to consider the tax implications of the option you choose so you know what you're getting yourself into.

If you work for the state, you may also have a drop program that allows you to continue working for 60 months while you take your retirement. This allows you to build your pension higher and accumulate more in your retirement plan.

When you're deciding which payout option to choose for your pension, I'm of the mindset that anytime you leave, you should take your money with you. Meaning, when you leave your job, whether it's a government job or a corporate job, it's better to put your money under your control than leave it under the control of the organization you worked for.

In the corporate world, if you get laid off, it's because the company is trying to downsize or reduce its finances. If you get laid off and leave your money with the corporation, there's a good chance you're not going to get your pension money—it doesn't belong to you until you sign the papers to retire. Because of this, when planning for retirement, many people decide to roll the pension into an IRA.

Most people don't realize how many places they have revenue coming in for retirement. They may have an annuity, a 401(k), an IRA, a pension, a retirement plan, life insurance with cash value, and more. Often, people have sources of income they haven't considered, such as child support, rental income from a property, or a life settlement from an insurance claim. When you plan for retirement, it's important to assess everything you have so you can create the best plan for distributing your assets.

## The Impact on Your Family

When you plan for retirement, it is more than just you who is impacted. Your spouse, kids, and other close relatives will be impacted by the decisions you make.

For instance, if you're planning for your kids to take care of you in the event that you become ill, incapacitated, or disabled, you need to have a conversation with them about this. The last thing you want is for your kids to not have a plan when an unfortunate event happens, leaving them scrambling to decide what to do.

If you're married, it's important for you and your spouse to get on the same page about retirement decisions. The choices you make may impact your spouse's benefits or affect what happens financially for your spouse if you pass away first.

A new client came to my office seeking help. This gentleman had, without consulting a professional, taken a life settlement on his pension, which was his biggest asset. He made a mistake in doing this—he forgot to take his wife, who was nine years younger, into consideration. I told him that one of two things would happen:

1) He would pass away and not leave his wife anything or
2) He would use the money up at some point, and his wife would struggle, trying to get a job at a late age. From then on, our goal in creating his retirement plan was to remedy this mistake and provide for his wife.

Often, people such as this client make decisions about retirement prematurely or without much thought, and they don't realize the consequences that these decisions will have.

Because your retirement decisions affect not only you but your spouse and kids, that's all the more reason to not delay retirement planning and to work with a professional. Your own future—and the future of your loved ones—is at stake.

If you have a pile of mail sitting somewhere in your house that represents financial decisions you are afraid of making—whether it's around Social Security, Medicare, estate planning, taxes, retirement accounts, or anything else—I'm coming to your rescue. I wrote this book to help people like you cut through the stress and fear and take actionable steps toward planning for retirement.

In the following chapters, I'm going to make the complex simple. My goal is to educate you about the decisions you will have to make so you are informed and empowered to begin the retirement planning process.

By the end of this book, my hope is that you'll be able to tackle that pile of mail once and for all. With a plan in place, you can finally stop worrying about retirement and start getting excited to enjoy your "golden years" with the ones you love.

In Chapter 2, I'll introduce you to the simple, 4-step process that makes this possible…

## CHAPTER 2

# From Engineering to Finance

*"The secret of getting ahead is getting started."*

–Mark Twain

Before we go any further, I want to tell you a little bit about my journey...

When I was young, my father handed me a small mortgage and finance book. We were having an important conversation about my goals for the future, and my father gave me some words of wisdom: "Son, this book will teach you how the strategy of compound interest will play against you when you owe money. However, it will also work the same way for you when you save money." My dad educated me on the importance of paying for things as I earned the money to buy them, not financing them and paying that compound interest to someone else. I studied that little book for months... I didn't know it at the time, but this moment planted the seed of my future career as a financial advisor.

On my father's advice, I decided to pursue a career in industrial engineering. Alongside industrial engineering, I also had the opportunity to study computer programming, which wasn't taught in most colleges back in 1969. After I completed my studies, I was asked to join a local lumber and hardware company. After six months, I was transferred to the company's headquarters to put my computer skills to work. As I completed my fifth year at this company, a major computer company spotted my work, and they offered me a position as an engineering technician at a major Fortune 500 company.

I bought my first home, married my beloved wife, and became a proud father to two sons. The next period of my life was filled with all of the struggles of balancing parenthood and a career, but they were filled with happy memories of the loving family my wife and I built.

## A Focus on Putting Clients First, Always

So, how did I go from an engineer to a financial advisor?

In 1991, I was chatting with my next-door neighbor, who was an insurance agent, by the mailbox about finances. At the end of the conversation, he said, "You know, it sounds like you're really passionate about this… Have you ever considered a career in financial services?" He sponsored me to get my first financial planning license, and a new chapter of my life began. I was most excited about the potential to help hardworking people manage their finances and build secure futures for their families.

At this point in life, I had years of experience in systems engineering and project management roles, including with some Fortune 500 companies such as Unisys Corp and Johnson Controls. My growing interest in transitioning to a career in financial services came at the right time… After a merger, the company I worked for began downsizing. Every Tuesday, there would be layoffs, and if you got a page on your pager at 7am, you knew it would be your last day. There were 17 of us who worked in a group, and I was the last one standing besides my boss. I knew my time would come eventually…

So, I started studying to finish my financial credentials. By the time my pager went off in 1992, my credentials were done. Within an hour after being laid off, I went to the Prudential office, began my career as a financial planner, and never looked back.

At first, I built my business on helping my peers who had been laid off. I helped them move their 401(k)s and take control of their retirement portfolios. I became a fiduciary early in my career, though this designation was less common then than it is now, since the Department of Labor has mandated financial institutions to be fiduciaries. For those who don't know, the definition of a fiduciary means that you are legally bound to act in the best interest of your client. To me, that was a no-brainer. I entered this business to help people.

In April of 2005, my Office of Supervision Jurisdiction (OSJ) asked me to freeze my book of business and only service my existing clients. They wanted me to focus on portfolio management, which consisted of creating plans, allocating investment positions for all of the financial advisors at the firm, and occasionally meeting with clients to explain the investment plans I created. Alongside this role, I also performed the duties of the Chief Compliance Officer, compelled to teach and monitor all advisors' actions and practices to ensure they were ethical and in accordance with industry regulations. Due to my engineering experience, I also became responsible for taking care of HVAC, computer, and fire inspection duties at the office.

While I was glad that my varied skills could be useful, I truly missed working with clients. I entered the financial services industry to help people, and I wanted to return to a more client-focused role as an advisor.

In June of 2009, I got an offer from a separate broker-dealer to manage the office and serve as the corporate principal. Here, I would review and sign off on several hundred stockbrokers' and financial advisors' trades, as well as daily paperwork that was submitted to the home office. This position led me to become the firm's National Sales Manager. As National Sales Manager, I was provided the opportunity to build a national supervision team. I took the opportunity to recruit several very experienced financial advisors from my previous firm and to provide a hierarchy network of supervision nationwide.

It was with this firm that I became extremely acquainted with our industry's regulators (FINRA), as I managed several of my supervisors from Kansas City to New York and was responsible for several of our firm's branches from California to Florida. It was a huge task, working with our firm's CEO and Chief Compliance Officer, along with coordinating all of the nationwide supervisors to ensure that each of our several hundred stockbrokers and a few financial advisors' practices were compliant according to industry regulations. I was privileged to meet with the regulator's enforcement team quite often, on behalf of the firm, my supervisors, and our brokers and advisors.

It was these experiences of dealing with many unruly brokers and advisors that made me realize I truly missed having my office and working with my clients. I reopened my office and continued to work with the people I loved the most.

Today, I am the President of Thomas Advisory Services, Inc. With over thirty plus years of experience as a financial advisor, I've helped countless individuals successfully retire. To this day, I'm proud of the fact that I put people first, and it is a joy to watch my clients retire knowing they'll have an income for life.

## It Doesn't Have to Be Complicated... And Shouldn't!

Because I have a background as an engineer, I naturally look for ways to make things more organized. When I entered the financial services industry, I began looking at ways to make the process, which can often be complex, more simple and organized for my clients. This led me to create The Four Pillars of Retirement Planning.

### Pillar 1: Organization

In this step, I need to learn as much about a client as I possibly can. I like to make this step feel like my client and I are just two friends sitting down for a cup of coffee. We'll explore the goals, responsibilities, and struggles that this client has in life. What is important to this person? What life goals do their finances support? Who are the people they care about and support financially? What concerns and fears do they have about their financial future?

At the end of this stage, we'll get organized. We'll turn the "never-ending pile of mail" into a file folder of important documents. This will give us a strong foundation to move forward and begin the financial planning process. We will discuss this in more detail in Chapter 3.

### Pillar 2: Debt Analysis

Once my client and I feel comfortable with each other, and once I understand this person's values, goals, and concerns, it's time to look at the facts. This begins with understanding the person's debt, or how much they need to spend each month. We'll assess spending in a variety of categories and calculate how much the person will need to live each month in retirement. We will cover this topic more in Chapter 4.

### Pillar 3: Asset Consolidation

What do you have and where do you have it? In this step, we uncover all of the assets a client has and form a clear picture of what we can use to create a retirement income. I will walk you through this pillar in Chapter 5.

### Pillar 4: Retirement Income

Now, we'll come up with a strategic plan that provides a guaranteed income for retirement. Once we know someone's assets and debts, we can determine how the person will draw from these assets so they don't outlive their money. Here, we'll also tackle important decisions about Social Security, Medicare, and more. We will explore this and more in Chapter 6.

With these Four Pillars, I'm able to turn the often complex process of financial planning into a simple, streamlined experience that helps clients achieve their financial and life goals.

**If you'd like to learn more about Thomas Advisory Services and the Four Pillars, please visit the following link to watch a video about our process:** https://creativeone.wistia.com/medias/odgryxnicj

# CHAPTER 3

# Getting Organized

In this chapter, we're going to cover Pillar 1: Organization. This is the first step to getting your finances in order and preparing for the future.

## Sorting Through the Pile of Mail

When a new client tells me they have a "never-ending pile of mail" somewhere at home, I tell them to bring it to me. Together, we rip open each envelope and find out what we have on our hands. We sort the mail into piles… Then, I tell the client to go get some lunch and come back in an hour.

When the client is gone, I go to the store and pick out the most colorful plastic file box I can find. Back at the office, I label each file… Auto insurance, home insurance, life insurance, utility bills, and so on. By the time my client gets back from lunch, the "never-ending pile of mail" has been transformed into an organized file box that is color-coordinated and labeled. We throw out all of the "junk mail" that doesn't belong in the box, and we pay any bills that are due.

Now, the client has a system to file away any new mail that comes in, and they can say goodbye to having that pile of mail cluttering up the counter. If a piece of mail comes in that they don't know what to do with, I'm one call away and can guide the client through the process of dealing with it. Over time, they tend to get the hang of it, and they can take care of business seamlessly, without having to ask questions.

I even go so far as to make an "index" of what each folder category is. That way, if the client goes out of town and needs to take care of something financial, I can tell them on the phone, "Go to folder #20. That's where we put the document you need." Having this system removes the panic and fear that most people face when they aren't sure how to handle something in their financial world.

This paper approach can be translated into digital files as well. You should have common namings across the physical and digital copies so it is easy for you to find everything—and easy for your spouse and kids to find everything in case you become incapacitated.

Are you ready to finally tackle your pile of mail?

Here are some easy action steps that will make this process painless:

1) Buy a filing folder.
2) Sort the mail by company, asset, etc.
3) Open each piece of mail, throw out the "junk," and file the rest in the proper folder.

When you accomplish these three simple steps, you can then take that folder to a financial planner, who will be able to quickly see what needs to be taken care of now that your papers are organized in one place. (Plus, you'll no longer have to look at that stressful pile of mail cluttering up the counter!) Once you take this first step to organize your finances, you'll build momentum and gather the courage to finally tackle planning for retirement. The first step is often the hardest to take, but once you take it, it will get easier.

**Prep for Your Taxes All Year**

When you have your financial paperwork organized, it streamlines your tax preparation.

I don't do taxes in April. I do taxes every day of the week.

Every time something comes in that has to do with taxes, it goes into the taxes file. This is the approach I try to teach my clients. That way, we can keep everything ready for your CPA and enrolled agent.

For instance, the moment you get a 1099, you would put it into your taxes file. If you buy a stock for $100 and sell it for $200, you need that 1099 to give the IRS confirmation that you bought it for $100. Otherwise, when you sell it, the IRS will only see that you had a gain of $200 because they can't confirm what you bought it for. Keeping your taxes organized ensures that you won't have to pay taxes on something you've already paid taxes on.

As you can see, Organization is a key element to building a plan for your financial future. Now that we've completed Pillar 1, we're going to move on to Pillar 2: Debt Analysis.

## CHAPTER 4

# Debt Analysis

*"The plans of the diligent lead surely to abundance, but everyone who is hasty comes only to poverty."*

–Proverbs 21:5

Many retirees tell me, "I'm afraid that I'll run out of money in retirement. What will happen if I outlive my money?"

If you retire without having enough assets to cover your debts, you'll have to return to work at some point so you don't run out of money.

Before you retire, each month you have money coming in and money going out. Our challenge in retirement planning is to ensure you will still have money coming in, though you will no longer have a paycheck from your job. However, you will still have money going out.

We'll cover how we're going to replace your income later, but we can't do that until we figure out how much money is going out each month. This is your debt, or the amount you need to spend each month to cover your expenses.

By the time you get ready to retire, if you don't know what you're spending each month, it's not time to retire…

Still, many people want to skip this part and focus on the question, "How much money do I need to retire?" These folks feel like there is a "magic number" they should have saved before retirement, and they want to know what this number is.

I'll tell you right now: the magic number is the amount that will allow you to cover your debts each month, for the rest of your life. That number may be higher or lower depending on the person.

It doesn't matter how much money you have if you can't pay your bills. You might think at first glance that someone who retires with a $5 million portfolio is better prepared than someone who retires with a $1 million portfolio. However, we have to take each person's debts into account. The person with $5 million may have exorbitant living expenses and spend above their means—that $5 million may not be enough to keep up. Meanwhile, $1 million may be more than enough to cover that person's living expenses. It's not about how much each person has in their portfolio… It's about whether that person has enough to cover what they are going to spend each month for the rest of their life.

You may be familiar with the 4% Rule, which is a rule of thumb that says a retiree should withdraw 4% of their retirement portfolio in the first year and then withdraw that dollar amount, adjusted for inflation, each year of retirement. While this is just a rule of thumb, and you should consult an advisor for individualized guidance, this rule can help give you an idea of how much you need in your portfolio.

You can divide the amount you spend each year by 0.04 to get the number you'd need to have in your portfolio before retirement.

For example, if you need $60,000 each year, you would divide that by 0.04 to get $1.5 million. In other words, $1.5 million is the amount this person needs to accumulate before retirement to ensure they won't run out of money if they spend $60,000 a year (which will adjust for inflation).

However, note that this rule does not take into account Social Security and pensions—having these cover some of your monthly expenses will lower the amount you'd need in a portfolio.

But as you can see, before you can begin estimating how much you'll need to retire, you need to know how much you spend each month.

That's where debt analysis comes in.

## Determining Your Monthly Spending

Because most people have the same bills, I created a template to help people identify their monthly expenses. These expenses can include:

- Groceries
- Eating/Take Out
- Gas/Electric
- Home Phone
- Water/Sewer
- Garbage
- Cable/Internet
- Lawn Care/Plants
- Pool Service
- Pest Control
- Security/Alarm
- Association Dues

- Clothing
- Hair Cuts
- Co-Pays/Deductibles
- Auto Gas
- Pet Care
- Tithing/Church
- Charity
- Car Payments
- Child Care
- Gym
- Car Repairs
- Car Maintenance
- Auto Insurance
- Travel/Vacation
- Home Repairs
- Furniture
- Gifts
- Cell Phone
- Credit Card (min.)
- Home Mortgage
- Subscriptions
- Kids' Sports
- Camps
- Student Loans
- Storage
- Miscellaneous
- Monthly Health Insurance Premiums
- Monthly Medical/ Dental/Vision Insurance Premiums
- Monthly Long-Term Care Insurance Premiums
- Monthly Disability Insurance Premiums
- Monthly Life Insurance Premiums
- Prescriptions

Take a moment to look at this list and calculate the amount you are confident you spend each month.

## Emergency Fund and Discretionary Fund

Now that you have a rough idea of your monthly spending, it's important to plan for your unexpected expenses, such as medical bills, home repairs, and any other emergency you can't predict.

I often say that retirement planning is about hoping for the best and preparing for the worst. One of the ways we prepare for the worst is by setting aside 4-6 months of living expenses as an emergency fund. It's important that this money is easily accessible to you so you can reach it in a time of need.

You never know when you're going to get sick or have an emergency, and the last thing you want is to have all of your money tied up in investments. A savings or money market account is usually a good place for an emergency fund. It may not be earning much, if any, interest, but that's okay. What's more important is that you know that you have the funds to take care of an emergency should one occur. A good advisor will understand the importance of keeping some money accessible for emergencies—if your advisor wants to invest all your money, that's not the right advisor.

After you have your emergency fund in place, you can start redirecting any excess funds into your discretionary fund and investment accounts so that your assets can have conservative growth over time.

Once you know how much your debt is, the next step is to analyze your assets. We'll cover this topic in the following chapter...

## CHAPTER 5

# Asset Accumulation and Consolidation

*"The first step in taking control of your financial life is to take stock of your current situation."*

–Suze Orman

Before you can plan for retirement, you have to know what you have and where you have it. In this chapter, we'll explore how to assess what assets you have so you and your advisor can use this information to make decisions about your future.

If you are still in the accumulation phase, you can work backward, using the monthly spending total you calculated in the last chapter to determine how much you need to cover this spending during your retirement. You can then strategize on how to best maximize your assets during the accumulation phase to reach this goal.

### What Do You Have and Where Do You Have It?

To begin this process, dig out all of your financial paperwork and take a look at everything you have. Hopefully, now that you've completed the organization process, this means pulling out your file folder in which everything is sorted and easy to find.

First, find your tax returns. Your tax returns will provide helpful "clues" about what you have and where you have it. Even if you forget about an asset, the IRS won't… You'll get a 1099 for it, even if you lost track of that particular investment. Often, clients are surprised when I tell them they have investments they completely forgot about: "Hey, where is this railroad stock your tax return says you have?"

"Oh my gosh! That was my grandfather's stock…" the astonished client will say, having no idea that they've been paying taxes on Grandpa's railroad stock for years.

Just last year, a client found out his grandparents left him an apartment when he got a 1099 in the mail—he would have had no idea otherwise. The checks had been direct deposited into his account once a month, so he didn't notice them. You'd be surprised how many people discover assets they either forgot about or inherited from family members (and have been unknowingly paying taxes on) when they take a closer look at their tax returns.

Usually, just the last two or three years of tax returns can give you the information you need to get started. Looking at these tax returns, make a list of what they say you have, and then track down paperwork for all of these assets.

Once you know what you have, you can address questions such as whether the asset is qualified or non-qualified. Qualified plans, such as 401(k)s, receive certain tax benefits because they are provided by employers to employees. Other qualified plans, such as IRAs, are provided by financial institutions.

How many checking and savings accounts do you have? Sometimes, clients come in with multiple checkbooks.

"Why do you have all of those?" I ask.

"Well, this one was my mom's, this one was my dad's, this one is for my daughter, this one is for my son..."

If this sounds like you, it's time to simplify and consolidate these accounts to make your life easier, especially as you begin to transition into retirement.

Your goal should be to have one sheet of paper that shows a "snapshot" of everything you own. This should give you a clear portfolio analysis and help you determine your net worth. Having this sheet that shows you the important information at a glance will help remove the stress and worry of having paperwork scattered everywhere and not knowing for certain what assets you have.

## Knowing Your Net Worth

When you sit down with a financial advisor, if you know what you have and where you have it, you'll be able to tell the advisor your liquid net worth, your non-liquid net worth, and your total net worth.

Your liquid net worth is made up of the assets you can use for your discretionary fund. On the other hand, your non-liquid net worth is made up of assets such as real estate. Once we have a clear picture of what your net worth is in each category, we can make decisions about what to do with these assets to accomplish your financial goals.

Knowing your net worth is important because some investment and retirement strategies are only available to you if you have a certain level of net worth. Additionally, your net worth may impact your tax and legacy planning.

When you're searching for a financial planner, knowing your net worth will also help you target a professional who typically works with people in your range. This will ensure that the advisor has experience implementing the appropriate strategies for your net worth and likely understands the mindset you have about money. (We'll cover choosing an advisor in more depth in Chapter 8).

## Tips for Accumulation for the Next Generation

Some of you reading this book might be Gen X, Millennials, or Gen Z, looking for strategies to secure your financial future as you accumulate assets. Or, as a Baby Boomer approaching retirement, you may be wondering what financial wisdom you can impart to set your kids and grandkids up for success.

Just as we discussed in the previous chapter, the basic formula to financial success is simple: calculate your monthly expenses, build an emergency fund that covers 4-6 months of expenses, and then put any "extra" money in a brokerage account or other investment so that your money can grow over time.

Using the Rule of 72, you can estimate the number of years required to double the money you invest at the annual rate of return:

**72 divided by *r* (the interest rate per period, as a percentage, not a decimal = *t* (the number of periods required to double an investment's value)**

If you invest $1,000 today at a 6% interest rate, using the Rule of 72 (72 divided by 6), it will take 12 years for that money to double to $2,000.

Because your money compounds over time, the earlier you start investing, the better. If you start thinking ahead to retirement as a young professional and understand the importance of investing your money today so it can grow, you'll set yourself up for success in the future.

Of course, there is no one-size-fits-all approach to finances, so you should consult a financial advisor for more complex and specific advice, but this basic framework is a good place to start.

What about the future of retirement planning?

Generation Z has heard over and over again that Social Security might not be around when they retire. According to the Social Security Administration, for someone with average earnings who retires in 2024 at age 65, Social Security benefits will replace 39%

of past earnings. If Social Security were to go away, that would mean the foundation of retirement planning for most people would no longer be there. Regardless of whether this will be true or not, the idea that Social Security will disappear is dangerous… As with most things in life, you have to prepare for the worst and hope for the best. I encourage young people to work hard and contribute to Social Security—if it is around when it's time for you to retire, you don't want to be left with no Social Security benefit or Medicare because you banked on these things going away. If it turns out that Social Security goes away, however, you can "prepare for the worst" by accumulating more assets throughout your life.

Younger generations are trending away from working for corporations, with many of them becoming small business owners or self-employed freelancers. This shift in the workforce will impact how financial planners encourage these folks to prepare for retirement, as the accumulation phase will look different for them than the traditional model of putting in time at a company and contributing to a 401(k). Since they will not have a 401(k) established automatically through a company they work for, people who are self-employed or business owners will have to be more intentional about setting up an account and putting money into it. If they are not intentional about saving for retirement, these people may not accumulate enough to hit their long-term goals because they did not have an employer setting this up for them.

There is also a generational difference in investments. Baby Boomers favor stocks and bonds, while Gen X favors investments they can touch and feel, such as real estate or gold and silver.

Gen Z is the opposite, investing in digital investments such as cryptocurrency. No matter what the generational trends and preferences for investments are, it's important for you to fully understand all of the options that are out there. Your retirement portfolio should be built around your specific goals and circumstances, not around whatever the "hot" investment is among your age group.

If you're a Baby Boomer reading this, I encourage you to be a financial role model to the next generation. You can lead by example, practicing good retirement planning habits that show your kids and grandkids how to be responsible with money. Have an open dialogue about the financial best practices you are learning, and encourage your relatives to save early.

If you're a younger person reading this, the best thing you can do is save and invest early so that your money can grow over time. Remember the Rule of 72... The earlier you start, the more your money will be able to compound. Your future self will thank you!

## The Sharebuilder's Program

One thing you may consider doing is starting a "Sharebuilder's program" within your family, whether for kids or grandkids. This is a custodian's account in a child's Social Security number that allows you to begin accumulating assets for the child's future while utilizing the tax advantages for minors. If you can get a life insurance policy for your kids, you can build equity in the policy that your kid can someday borrow against. Most parents help their kids financially from ages 18-25, whether supporting them through college or covering expenses while they secure their first job. With a life insurance policy in place, you create a fund that your kids can borrow from during this period when they are establishing themselves financially—and they can borrow against the insurance more cheaply than they could borrow at a bank. Essentially, you're putting money in a position for yourself and your kids that can accumulate in a tax-free environment where you can borrow at a small percentage of difference on the interest rate. If you don't borrow it, it accumulates on a tax-deferred basis. Later on, if you don't need the life insurance, you can automatically transfer it into an annuity that can give you a lifetime income.

The Sharebuilder's program is a great alternative to a college savings account. Every parent wants to set money aside to help their children prepare for the future. However, while decades ago, a college degree would secure a stable, well-paying job, these days, that isn't always the case. It's likely that we will see college degrees becoming less relevant in the future, especially as younger generations favor entrepreneurship and self-employment. It's best to save for your child's future in a way that could be applied to any path they take, whether that is a college degree, trade school, starting a small business, or pursuing a career field that prioritizes real-world experience over higher education.

Now that we've explored how to identify the assets you've accumulated (and how the next generation should approach the accumulation phase), let's investigate how these assets transition into retirement income.

## CHAPTER 6

# Retirement Income

*"Someone's sitting in the shade today because someone planted a tree a long time ago."*

–Warren Buffett

Now that you have an idea of the assets you have, it's time to explore how you will draw from these assets to create retirement income.

You now know how much your debt will be each month. First, you'll need to determine how much of that debt will be covered by Social Security (and any pensions you may have). Then, the remainder of that debt is how much you'll need to draw from your assets.

For example, a retiree named Lisa needs $4,000 each month to cover her expenses. She will receive $1,500 from Social Security each month and does not have a pension, so she will need to draw $2,500 each month from her assets.

Before retirement, most people have an idea in mind of where they will draw income from—but most people don't have a full understanding of how disbursements work. Whether they're planning to draw money out of a brokerage account, a 401(k), or something else, people usually don't take the sequence of distribution into consideration.

For instance, if you start drawing money out of your brokerage account when the market's going down, you're taking out money when your account should be growing back to where it was before the market went down.

The timing of withdrawing from your portfolio is crucial. If you draw from it when the market is up, you won't even notice the fact that you drew money out because your portfolio is replenishing itself.

On average, the market is usually at an 8.5% rate of return over a 20-year period, so most people feel comfortable drawing 4% from their portfolios. However, these people forgot one important variable: how long they will live. That's a big unknown... And there's no way to know the answer for sure, even if you make an educated guess based on your health and family history.

***Take a look at this retiree constantly having to watch the markets to ensure his retirement income will cover his bills each month. Is this how you want to spend your retirement?***

## A Guaranteed Income for Life

When your money runs out, do you still want to get paid? If the answer is yes (I've never met anyone who said no), we need to guarantee the amount of money you need to pay the bills each month. There's only one way to guarantee anything in the financial business, and that's with insurance. If you use the word guaranteed in securities, they'll lock you up. But in insurance, you can use the word guaranteed because they can actually guarantee your assets. In a fixed index annuity, your principal is guaranteed not to go down below 0, even in a down market. In a down market, your principal may not increase, but it won't go below what last year's principal was, and it won't go below zero. Remember, "Zero is our hero." If we know zero is our hero, then everything above zero is available to be taken out. That provides us with a stable income. Zero is defined as your initial investment minus any rider costs.

With insurance, we can guarantee income for life, either for one spouse or two, depending on the income level and carrier.

Through debt analysis, we can determine if the revenue will be enough to cover the debt, and if it will not be enough, we need to put more money into the account. However, there is a limit to how much we can put in certain accounts, depending on the liquidity. We also need to ensure that you have 4-6 months of emergency funds that cannot be tied up in non-liquid accounts.

In summary, you want to draw your retirement income from a guaranteed account, which involves insurance. With a guaranteed account, you know with certainty that you will have an income for life in retirement and will have enough money to cover your expenses each month as long as you live.

***Compare the fixed index annuity retirement plan to this stock market trend of market swings. Is this what you want your retirement balance and income to be based upon? Yes, there's an upward trend, but there are ups and downs constantly. Will it be up or down on the day your income is distributed to you? There's no guarantee...***

Once your guaranteed account has enough in it to cover your debt, the remainder of your assets will be placed in a discretionary account, which is a conservative portfolio that will grow to provide you with funds to draw from in an emergency (in addition to your 4-6 month emergency fund). We want this to be a conservative portfolio because we don't want to lose principal, even though we can't guarantee this.

One thing I try to stress with all of my clients is that if you have a guaranteed income for life on a fixed index annuity, you might as well start taking it as soon as the amount every month is enough to live on. Even if the cash value runs out, you'll still get a check. The sooner you take it, the sooner you'll be living on the insurance money and not your own money.

To put it simply, if you draw from a brokerage account, you could run out of money. If you draw from a guaranteed account, you'll get a check even if you run out of money.

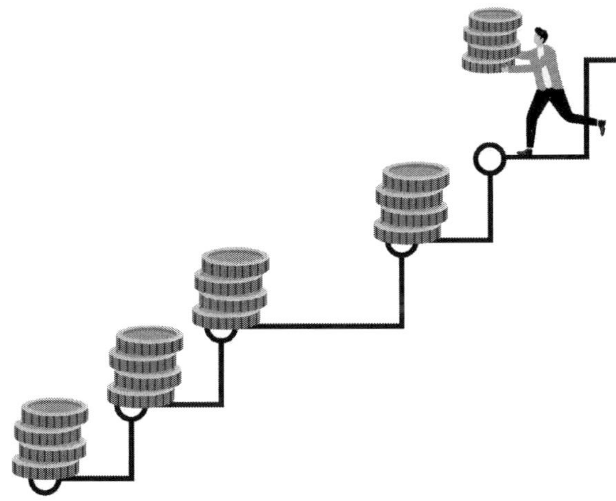

***A safe retirement with the use of fixed index annuities, guarantees income for life, and no market losses. If the market drops below your last anniversary date, then there is no interest earned but no loss of your account balance. If the market increases above your last anniversary date, then interest will be applied to your account balance.***

## When Should I Take Social Security?

Social Security's role in your retirement plan depends on the age you want to retire. Knowing the age you want to retire, you can go on the Social Security website, enter your Social Security number, and find out exactly how much you're going to receive depending on the age you retire.

At this point, you should know how much money you will need each month, and you can calculate how much income you'll need in addition to Social Security to cover your monthly expenses. Social Security will make up the first part of your retirement income, and you'll supplement it with the guaranteed income that we discussed in the previous section.

But most people don't realize that every year above their normal retirement age that they do not take their Social Security, the benefit increases by 8%. For example, if your normal retirement age is 66, if you delay taking Social Security for four years, your benefit will increase by 8% a year. When you turn 70 and begin taking Social Security, you will be able to draw an income that is a 32% increase of your normal retirement benefit.

However, note that if you wait to take Social Security until you're 71, you don't get that extra 8%. You're only going to get 8% a year for 48 months maximum, up to age 70. Essentially, there's no reason for anyone to wait to take Social Security past age 70.

Delaying taking Social Security increases your benefit, yet it is not the right decision for everyone. To determine whether it is more beneficial to take Social Security at your normal retirement age or later, we can calculate how many years it would take you to break even if you delay taking it.

For most people, it will take 12-14 years. If you take Social Security at age 70, this would mean you'll be 82-84 before you break even. If you pass away prior to that age, you might as well take Social Security at the normal retirement age. If you have health conditions or family history that make it likely you will pass away earlier, that may factor into your decision.

Not only will the government give you an 8% benefit for each year that you wait, but they will also reduce your benefit if you take Social Security early. For a person born in 1957 and considering starting Social Security at age 62 or so, there is a reduction of about 27.5% for starting Social Security early. This reduction is not a penalty. Many people who want to retire early change their minds when they realize their Social Security benefit will be reduced.

## Be Careful as You Draw Down

Once you establish a plan for drawing income in retirement, it's important not to sabotage your plan by making mistakes…

As you're drawing income in retirement, it's important to pay attention to your spending so you don't go over the projected monthly spending you planned for. If your spending changes beyond what you and your advisor planned for, you will have to draw down faster, meaning you may have to adjust the risk tolerance in your discretionary account or pull more out of your annuity prematurely.

Once you're retired, resist the temptation to rack up credit card debt on unnecessary purchases. If you spend too much in one area, cut back on spending in another area so you can stick to your budget and avoid having to change your retirement plan.

Your advisor is responsible for managing your assets, but you are more responsible for managing your debt. A good advisor should provide guidance on managing your debt and help you practice good spending habits, but at the end of the day, your advisor won't be standing next to you at the cash register every time you make a purchase. It's up to you to know your number and stick to it so you can have confidence in your retirement.

Another mistake retirees often make is taking money out of their qualified account, not realizing that the qualified account has penalties and surrender charges, some of which could be up to 20%... It's imperative that you talk to your advisor before you call the insurance company and ask for withdrawals so they can prevent you from making this mistake.

## Case Study: Jane and Bob

My clients, a couple who I'll call Jane and Bob, came into my office thinking they could retire tomorrow.

Though Bob owned a successful company and the couple owned their home, they didn't have any assets accumulated... And when we went through Pillar 2: Debt Analysis, we discovered that Bob and Jane's debt was way above their income.

Bob and Jane's retirement goal didn't match their reality. As an advisor, my task was to help Bob and Jane get as close to what they wanted, which was retiring as soon as they could, while ensuring they would have enough retirement income to live comfortably for the rest of their lives.

Bob wanted to sell the business, hoping that doing so would provide additional assets for retirement. However, I helped the couple understand why this was a bad idea. The business was Bob and Jane's source of revenue, and they needed that revenue to pay off the debt. I determined that Bob and Jane needed to keep running the business for 3-5 more years before they could retire. After that, we would maximize the zone of opportunity and figure out the most advantageous time to sell the business.

Essentially, our plan was:

1) Pay down debt
2) Increase revenue
3) Maximize the sale of the business

Once Bob and Jane understood the reality of the situation, they were okay with working a few more years, knowing that doing so would ensure they could remain successfully retired.

This is just one example of how advisors navigate each retiree's unique financial situation and help them get as close to the target as possible.

# CHAPTER 7

# Other Retirement Considerations

*"Planning is about bringing the future into the present so you can do something about it now."*

–Alan Lakein

In this chapter, we're going to examine some of the other factors you need to consider as you plan for retirement…

## Long-Term Care

Long-term care is one of the considerations that people put off thinking about or forget about altogether. Most people don't realize the importance of planning for long-term care until they have to put their elderly parents in a facility or take care of them at home.

Additionally, most people don't realize the cost of long-term care insurance… When I give a quote to my clients, they just about choke on the number.

It can be sticker shock, but remember that the cost of paying out-of-pocket for long-term care is much, much higher. According to Genworth, the median cost of a private room in a nursing home is $10,025 per month in 2024. The cost of long-term care is rising faster than inflation. It can take up all of your discretionary money… And if you fail to prepare for long-term care, your kids may have to leave their jobs or pay out of their own pockets to hire a full-time or part-time caretaker for you.

One way to tackle paying for long-term care is through a hybrid life insurance or annuities investments. A hybrid is the cheapest way to ensure your senior care because if you don't use it, you don't lose it. The money will just go to something else, whether it is put back into your retirement funds or passed to your heirs. With a traditional long-term care policy, if you don't use the insurance before you pass away, that money is gone.

With a hybrid life insurance policy, there is no extra charge (on most carriers) for long-term care insurance, and you will see on your statement how much money is allocated for your long-term senior care.

When it comes to long-term care insurance, you're going to pay the same amount of money, no matter if you get insurance early or late. You will pay more per month for insurance the later you get it. However, because you will be paying for more months if you get it early, it evens out, meaning there is not an advantage either way to getting it early or late—other than the peace of mind of knowing that your long-term care is covered. Because it doesn't matter too much when you get this insurance, and because of how expensive it can be, this is usually something people purchase when they can afford it, after they have paid off the mortgage and supported the kids through college. Once all of your other major life expenses are behind you, you can turn your focus to saving for senior care.

It's important to note that when you start taking senior health care benefits off of a life insurance policy or annuity, it adds to the amount of income you have every year, which might disqualify you from Medicaid. That's something to factor into your discussions with your advisor about planning for long-term care.

## Medicare

When you begin thinking about Medicare, one of the first questions to consider is, "What is your health status?"

How often do you get sick? Do you have a family history of cancer, heart attacks, strokes, or other health issues?

I have some clients who have never taken a pill, and other clients who can't stay out of the hospital. No matter where you fall on this spectrum, we need to structure your Medicare properly so it meets your unique health needs.

If you never get sick, and you structure your Medicare with the assumption that you will be healthy, if you do get sick down the road, it will surprise you. This will mess up your overall retirement plan because you will have to spend more than you planned and draw more from your portfolio. So, when it comes to Medicare, we want to plan for the worst and hope for the best.

When you retire, you're approaching the period of life when most people, even if they have been healthy their whole lives, will get sick. You need to have a plan for that.

One of the decisions you'll need to make is whether to do a Medicare Advantage plan or a Medicare Supplement. Either way, you will will need to do the prescription plan. A Medicare Advantage plan includes Medicare Parts A, B, C, and D. A Medicare Supplement is secondary to original Medicare.

Medicare Supplement typically comes with higher premiums but lower out-of-pocket costs, while Medicare Advantage usually comes with lower premiums but more out-of-pocket costs.

I've met many clients who want to take the easy way out on premiums and then complain when they don't pay off. Medicare Advantage plans are getting much better, but they're not known to pay for everything. Don't be lured in by an Advantage plan that has no premiums… As the saying goes, "You get what you pay for."

If you have a heart attack and go to the hospital, with a Medicare Advantage plan, you might end up paying 50% of your medical costs if you are not within your network. Meanwhile, with a Medicare Supplement, Medicare will pay for any medical costs that are reasonable and customary, and you don't have to be in your network—it could be any network in the country, and sometimes even out of the country.

## Life Insurance

If you have people in your life who are dependent on you, you need life insurance. If you pass away, life insurance will replace your income so that your spouse and kids can continue the same lifestyle they had while you were alive.

For instance, imagine you have a mortgage. When you pass away, if your spouse isn't able to pay for the mortgage alone, what would happen to your family?

Or, if you have kids attending college, and your income is funding their education, what would happen if you passed away and they lost this support?

Life insurance is a tool designed to protect the people you love.

Beyond being a tool to replace your income should you pass away, life insurance can also be used strategically when we are planning for retirement. You can overfund a life insurance policy to a certain level, called a 7-year level pay, and it will not be taxed upon your withdrawal. The loans you can take from your life insurance will be much cheaper than loans you can take from the bank, and you can use the money in your life insurance policy as collateral. You can also use the death benefit while you're alive instead of after you're gone, meaning you could use it to fund senior care. The carriers will not allow your policy to go below a certain amount, usually $15,000-$20,000, so that your life insurance policy will cover your funeral, but otherwise, you can use your death benefit to cover the costs of retirement while you are alive.

## Estate Planning

The death tax is constantly changing, and it's getting ready to change again.

The average person won't have an estate tax problem. Currently, you can pass on up to about $6 million of assets per spouse in your estate plan tax-free. However, this is based on who is in Congress and what policies are passed.

When thinking about estate plans, we need to know your total net worth and what is in your portfolio. This is why it's so important to determine your net worth in earlier steps, when you are getting organized and understanding what assets you have.

If you do not have an estate plan, your estate will go through probate. When an estate goes through probate, there is a monetary cost, but I'm more concerned about the cost of time it takes to go through probate. Do you want your estate to go through probate, or do you want to control what happens to your assets?

Let's say a couple has a mortgage on their house, and eventually, they both pass away. Their estate, which they've left to their kids, passes through probate, which takes months or years. Meanwhile, the kids need to pay Mom and Dad's mortgage, but the money Mom and Dad left them to do so is frozen in probate. The kids may not have the money to afford Mom and Dad's lifestyle, so if they can't access these funds, they'll be in trouble.

One way we can avoid this problem is through life insurance. Life insurance can be used by beneficiaries within days of a death, so the kids can maintain Mom and Dad's mortgage without having to wait for probate.

**Another consideration of an estate plan: dependent care.**

One of my clients has an adult daughter with special needs, and they were worried about what would happen to her after they passed away, especially since they were growing older. They wanted their other daughter to take care of her sister, but they knew this wouldn't be feasible unless the daughter was provided with income so she could leave her job to be a full-time caregiver. Together, we created a special needs trust that would provide both daughters with enough income to allow one sister to care for the other. The trust also specified that the sister was to be the caregiver of the daughter with special needs and was to manage any funds that were left for her sister's care. Once this trust was created, the parents had peace of mind, no longer fearful about what would happen to their daughter when they passed away.

As you can see, there are many complexities to planning for retirement, some that most people don't think of. To ensure you're prepared for these complexities, it's crucial to have the right advisor on your team who can help you navigate these important decisions.

## CHAPTER 8

# Choosing the Right Advisor

> *"Listen to advice and accept discipline, and at the end you will be counted among the wise."*
>
> –Proverbs 19:20

When it comes time to choose an advisor, where do you begin?

Most people start by Googling financial advisors in their area. However, just because someone's name appears at the top of your Google search results, that does not mean they are necessarily the right advisor for you. It's important to take things a step further and interview your advisor by having an initial meeting.

In this initial meeting, just as you're interviewing your advisor, your advisor is interviewing you, determining if you're a right fit for his or her client list. Your relationship with a financial advisor should be a long-term, trusting relationship, so both parties should ensure that the relationship is the right fit before moving forward. Consider what questions the advisor is asking you and whether they are truly interested in getting to know you.

Meeting with an advisor is like meeting someone on a first date… On a first date, you usually know if you're comfortable talking to someone after just a few minutes, and it's the same with a potential financial advisor. Right off the bat, you will get a sense of if you like this person, if you get along, if you would feel comfortable talking about your finances and personal life circumstances with this person, and if you would trust this person to help you make important decisions. If you answer "yes" to all of those questions, you will want to talk to the advisor again, and after meeting a few times, a relationship will begin to form.

As you can see, choosing the right advisor is not about "can this person make me money" or "what returns will this person get me." There are plenty of capable advisors who can handle the mechanics of your finances, so choosing the right advisor is more about a relationship with two people. Your advisor will guide you through decisions for decades, and they will be there during difficult and important moments in your life to provide advice and take care of business. Do you like this advisor's communication style? Does their personality make you feel comfortable when you step into their office?

Money can be a personal topic, especially when you're discussing uncomfortable subjects like long-term care or estate planning. The last thing you want is an advisor you feel nervous or intimidated to open up to as you're making these important decisions. You should enjoy spending time with your advisor! If you have to have a lifelong relationship with someone, it might as well be someone you enjoy talking to and can have positive, friendly conversations with.

You can tell a good advisor based on their way of life. If they are living the way you are living, this is probably a suitable match. If an advisor is living above your income range, this may not be the right fit—this advisor may charge higher fees tailored to a wealthier clientele, and the approach to managing money might be tailored to this clientele as well.

When you've identified an advisor you're interested in, you can visit BrokerCheck.org to see this advisor's history and any potential red flags.

**A Great Advisor Helps You Accomplish Your Goals**

While this chapter focuses on considerations for choosing an advisor, I want to share a brief story about the benefits of having a relationship with an advisor. Once you have this partnership, you know that you have a trusted guide to call upon each time you need to make a financial decision. With your advisor's expert guidance, you can make more strategic decisions that allow you to accomplish your goals.

A year ago, I received a call from a client asking for my advice on how to sell a piece of real estate without paying a large capital gains tax on the sale. So, we scheduled a time to meet and review his options. As we met and discussed the possibility of a 1031 exchange, my client received a call from a gentleman who wanted to sell a tract of land that adjoined my client's residence. I recommended that I assist them both in performing a 1031 exchange so they could each save hundreds of thousands of dollars in capital gains taxes.

Once this was agreed upon, I connected with my qualified intermediary (QI) and we used his services for both parties' transactions.

As the transactions progressed, it was decided that my client wanted to purchase the tract of land adjoining his residence with the funds from the sale of his real estate. Also, the seller of the tract of land had a goal of investing his proceeds into income-producing investments and using part to purchase a house for his daughter and the rest to use for their travel plans.

After the required timeframe, my client sold his real estate, and the funds were transferred directly to the seller's QI escrow account for the purchase of the tract of property adjoining my client's residence. By handling these transactions in such a way that neither seller took receipt of any of the funds, no capital gains taxes were required to be paid until future sales occurred, or the investments distributed any income to the seller.

Now that both transactions have been completed, additional investments have been made, and income has been distributed, both clients are ecstatic about how their goals were accomplished. My client has begun to improve his newly acquired tract of land, and the seller has provided the necessary funds to his daughter and concluded one of his many travel plans.

As a financial advisor, helping my clients use financial strategies to accomplish their goals, and seeing them satisfied with the outcomes of their decisions, gives me great pleasure.

## What Does the Advisor Charge?

After you've confirmed that this is an advisor you trust and could see yourself having a long-term relationship with, the next step is to understand how the advisor charges.

Do they charge a flat fee? Do they charge a percentage of assets managed? Fiduciaries are required to charge a percentage of assets managed and in your best interest.

Financial advisors are required to provide you with an ADV Part 2, a document that tells you about the advisor, how much they can charge, and whether or not they can charge commissions in addition to fees.

How are your bills to the financial advisor going to get paid? Usually, commissions are paid by the insurance carrier, not by the client. Asset fees are typically taken out of the client's brokerage account automatically. If the client doesn't have a brokerage account with the advisors firm, then an invoice would be provided.

## Credentials

There are a lot of credentials that financial advisors could potentially have, so it's important to understand what they mean and which ones matter.

The CFP (Certified Financial Planner) designation is about ethics. Most advisors want to obtain this designation, but personally, in the last 20 of my 32 years in the business, I no longer see the value in it. I've seen people with the CFP designation take part in unethical behavior, so I'm no longer confident that this designation makes a difference in whether a financial advisor will make ethical or unethical choices. However, the CFP designation has recently been advertised on television, so many clients are led to believe that they need a financial advisor with this designation.

So, if a financial advisor has the CFP designation, don't take this as a face-value sign that they are an ethical advisor. Do your due diligence by reading their reviews and investigating how they charge fees—this will tell you more about the advisor's ethics than the CFP designation will.

Credentials are important to a degree, but what is more important is the relationship between you and a potential advisor. Most designations teach roughly the same thing, so often, they don't indicate a major difference in the advisor's approach… It just means that the advisor read a book and passed a test. I once knew an advisor who had about six designations behind his name, yet he rarely met with his clients… He only knew what he had read about financial planning, but he didn't know how to translate his book smarts into the real world and help people.

In my opinion, what the advisor has done for previous clients in the real world is a much better indication of quality than the amount of letters they have after their name. If you can, see what previous clients are saying about the advisor and how he or she impacted the client's life… They don't hand out designations for each client an advisor helps successfully retire, but the truest sign of an advisor's merit is the lives they have changed.

## Succession Planning

What is the size of the advisor's team, and what is their succession plan?

The last thing you want is for your advisor to pass away or retire with no succession plan, leaving your financial future at stake.

The most senior advisors with the most expertise and experience in the field are going to be older people. Many of them (myself included) could retire tomorrow if they wanted to, yet choose to stay in the business past retirement age because they have a passion for helping people.

Older advisors are often great choices because they bring decades of experience to the table, yet it's important to have an open conversation about the advisor's succession plans so you can ensure your financial plan will continue in trusted hands if the advisor eventually retires or passes away before you do.

For instance, I have a strong back-of-house team, as well as a son who has the credentials, experience, and desire to take over my firm. The day I retire, my clients will experience a seamless transition, and their financial plans will continue full speed ahead. Personally, I have so much love for this business and my clients that I don't want to retire until I have to, but it's important to me to have this succession plan lined up to protect my clients in case the unexpected happens.

Does your potential advisor have a plan like this in place?

## Faith and Core Principles

Earlier, I mentioned that the best advisor for you is likely one who is living the way you're living. I previously discussed this in relation to income bracket and financial lifestyle, but I want to take it a step further... The best advisor is one who shares your core values in life.

When you talk to an advisor who shares your core values, they will understand where you're coming from and why you want to make certain decisions.

For instance, if you're married with children and believe in family values, an advisor living a similar life will understand how important your family is to you and help you make financial decisions aligned with these values.

If you're a person of faith, the best advisor for you will be a person of faith. When you're aligned in your spiritual beliefs, your advisor will help you make decisions in accordance with these beliefs. Because you share common ground on your most deeply-held values, it will be easier to have deeper conversations about your financial goals and how you can use your money in a God-honoring way. However, you want to avoid advisors who seem like they're insincere in their beliefs or only using their faith as a marketing tactic.

As a Christian myself, I gravitate towards clients who are fellow Christians. My clients are a direct reflection on my reputation, and I don't want to work with someone who is going to be in and out of trouble—that would affect the way people see me. I don't want to work with clients who love money more than God. I didn't enter the financial industry because I love money and growing money for money's sake. I entered the financial industry because I love people, and I want to help people use their money in a way that helps them live joyous, God-honoring lives, support their families, and give to charity.

Because I am a Christian, I can help other Christians make decisions about money that are aligned with Christian beliefs. For instance, some clients don't want to invest money in alcohol, tobacco, or firearms, so I can guide them to investments that honor God.

Outside of financial decisions, I always enjoy the spiritual conversations I have with my Christian clients over the years, and it strengthens our relationship when we're able to bond over our shared faith.

So, I encourage you to find an advisor who shares your values so you can build a lifelong, trusting relationship and together, plan for a financial future that aligns with your beliefs.

In summary, here is a checklist of what to consider when looking for a financial advisor:

- Do you feel comfortable when talking to this advisor?
- Do you like the advisor's communication style?
- Does the advisor often work with people with your net worth?
- Have you visited BrokerCheck.org to verify that there are no red flags about the advisor?
- How does the advisor charge fees?
- What are previous clients saying about the advisor in reviews and testimonials?
- Does the advisor have a strong succession plan in place?
- Is your advisor aligned with your faith and core principles?

When you find the right advisor, you can finally put a retirement plan into place and let go of your worries about the future.

# CHAPTER 9

# Simplify Your Life

*"The best time to plant a tree was twenty years ago. The second best time is now."*

–Chinese proverb

We're nearing the end of our journey together in this book. I hope I've opened your eyes to the need to be prepared in your financial life so you can create a secure future for yourself and the ones you love.

When you simplify your life, you can focus on living it. Life should be fulfilling, rewarding, and joyful, spent honoring your beliefs and enjoying time with friends and family. Once you have a roadmap for your financial future and know that you have everything organized, you can let go of fear and worry and focus on what matters most.

I encourage you to "pay it forward" and pass on the information you've learned in this book to your family, friends, and neighbors. Everyone deals with worry around finances, and if this book can play a role in educating people so they no longer feel that worry, I will feel I've done my part. This book was born out of a lifetime of experiences as a financial advisor, and my goal in writing it was to give people a simple tool to understand the decisions they will one day face, whether that day is just around the corner or decades away.

Now, your next step is to find a financial advisor who aligns with your needs (see Chapter 8) and begin building your financial future.

However, there's a big mistake you need to avoid—resist the temptation to put down this book, thinking, "I'll get to it later." "Later" never comes… Months and years will go by, and eventually, you'll forget that you needed to find a financial advisor. Like the majority of our population, you'll find yourself unprepared for the challenges and decisions in your financial future, and someday, you'll wish you had taken action earlier.

The earlier you start preparing for retirement, the more time you'll have to accumulate assets, and the more options you'll have available. Plus, you'll have more "worry-free" years of knowing that your retirement plan is already in place.

Take the first step today. No one ever regrets starting "too early"—but plenty of people regret starting too late.

## Tomorrow Is Not Promised…

Thirty years ago, in my second year in the business, I got a call from a business owner, John, who was a friend of my parents. John asked me to come down to his store and give him a quote for life insurance. It was the first week of the month, so when I got to the store, it was crowded with people using food stamps. I could hardly get in the door.

Because of the crowds, John wanted to talk to me in his air-conditioned Cadillac while we drove around the parking lot. I asked him why he called me up about life insurance, and through our conversation, I found that he was concerned about protecting his family and his business if he passed away unexpectedly.

I told him, "Why don't we put a policy on you that would be large enough to protect your family and your business, and let your business pay for it all?"

Over the next few weeks, I talked to corporate and got them to agree to pay John's premium. To finalize the policy, we only needed three things:

1) A signed application
2) A down payment
3) John needed to get a physical

I went back to the store, and John and his wife signed the application amidst all the shoppers checking out at the counter. They provided the down payment, and I got my doctor, whose office was about 3 miles away, to agree to stay open an hour later so John could come by and take a physical. We were all set to have the policy in place as soon as John took that physical.

But as I was leaving, John said, "You know what, let me do that physical on Monday."

I tried to convince him otherwise, but he was adamant that he didn't feel like going now and would take care of it on Monday.

I left town for a weekend trip with my sons, but early Saturday morning, my mother called me and said, "John passed away."

"John who?" I asked, in disbelief. It couldn't be the John I just saw yesterday, who was planning on getting a physical on Monday.

But it was… It turned out that after I left the store, John had gone home, had a heart attack, and passed away. Because he had not gotten a physical, his life insurance policy was never finalized.

John's wife got in touch with me on Monday morning, wanting to file a claim for John's death benefit, and I had to tell her that, unfortunately, John was not insured because he never got a physical.

I was shaken up, but I learned a lesson I will never forget… If someone wants or needs a life insurance policy, the policy should be put in place right away.

What's more, I learned from my parents that John's father had died of a heart attack at the same age. John had a twin brother, and as soon as I heard about his family history, I urged John's wife to tell her brother-in-law to get a life insurance policy right away.

I tell this story to remind you that tomorrow is not promised. None of us can predict when our time will come, but the best we can do for our loved ones is to **prepare as early as possible.**

# CONCLUSION

As you reach the end of this book, I hope you've come to see that retirement planning is about more than just saving money or choosing the right investments—it's about building a life of security, freedom, and fulfillment. By taking charge of your financial future, you're not only preparing to enjoy your retirement years; you're also creating a legacy for your family, shaping a meaningful future for yourself, and reducing the stress and uncertainty that can come with financial decisions. Now, equipped with knowledge, strategies, and a clear understanding of the steps you need to take, it's time to take the next step and seek out a financial advisor to guide you on your journey.

## It's Never Too Early...

When it comes to retirement, time is one of the most valuable resources you have. The sooner you start taking action, the more options you'll have and the less stress you'll experience as you approach your retirement years. Planning for retirement is not a one-time event—it's an ongoing process that benefits greatly from early, consistent attention. By taking action now, you'll be setting yourself up for a smoother journey and a better outcome. And, as you learned from John's story, none of us knows what tomorrow will bring. The opportunity to take control of your financial future is best seized today, before it's too late.

Life is unpredictable, and retirement comes with its own set of challenges—health concerns, market fluctuations, changes in Social Security, and unexpected expenses, to name a few. A comprehensive retirement plan, designed around The Four Pillars, will ensure you're prepared to face these uncertainties with confidence.

## A Secure Future for You and Your Loved Ones

Once the work of planning for retirement is complete, an extraordinary future awaits you…

It's my honor in life to help people just like you reach this future. Each time I help a client breathe a sigh of relief or realize their financial goals are within reach, I'm reminded of why my work is important. Each time I help a grieving family navigate a tricky financial situation or help a worried client overcome a struggle, I feel proud to be a financial advisor. And each time a client celebrates retirement after years of hard work, it fills me with joy.

I'm always eager to help more people organize their financial lives, and I'd like to make myself available to have a deeper conversation on any of the topics in this book. As I mentioned earlier, my Christian values are central to my life, and if you're a person of faith seeking a like-minded advisor, I would be happy to have a conversation.

If you'd like to learn more about Thomas Advisory Services, please scan the QR code below to visit our website.

# ABOUT THE AUTHOR

Since 1992, Allen Thomas has demonstrated excellence in providing clients with custom-tailored wealth management solutions. Allen is especially well-known for strategies focused on retirement income plans for individuals, estate and inheritance preservation planning, and small to medium-sized company retirement plans.

A native of Florida, Allen attended the College of Automation in Jacksonville, FL. He worked for several Fortune 500 companies, including Unisys Corp. and Johnson Controls in systems engineering and project management roles. Allen's financial services career began with Prudential Financial Services and has included management roles with several prominent firms, such as Boston-based Investors Capital and Lakeland, FL-based Brookstone Securities.

Allen and his wife, Kathy, an RN, reside in Winter Haven, Florida, and are actively involved in their church and several local charities.

Allen's achievements on affiliations include:

- FINRA Series 6 (Investment Company and Variable Contracts), FINRA Series 7 (General Securities Representative), FINRA Series 24 (General Securities Principal), FINRA Series 66 registration (investment advisor representative), FINRA Series 79 (Investment Banking Representative), and FINRA Series 99 (Operations Professional)
- Life, Health, Property/Casualty Insurance and Variable Annuities Licenses
- Member Polk Republican Executive Committee
- Member Polk County "CERT" Community Emergency Response Team
- Member Winter Haven Chamber of Commerce